The Presidency

KNOW YOUR GOVERNMENT

The Presidency

Christine Brendel Scriabine

CHELSEA HOUSE PUBLISHERS

Editor-in-Chief: Nancy Toff
Executive Editor: Remmel T. Nunn
Managing Editor: Karyn Gullen Browne
Copy Chief: Juliann Barbato
Picture Editor: Adrian G. Allen
Art Director: Giannella Garrett
Manufacturing Manager: Gerald Levine

Staff for THE PRESIDENCY

Senior Editor: Elizabeth L. Mauro
Associate Editor: Pierre Hauser
Assistant Editor: Michele A. Merens
Copyeditors: Terrance Dolan, Ellen Scordato
Editorial Assistant: Tara P. Deal
Picture Research: Dixon & Turner Research Associates
Designer: Noreen M. Lamb
Production Coordinator: Joseph Romano

Creative Director: Harold Steinberg

    3   5   7   9   8   6   4   2

Library of Congress Cataloging in Publication Data

Scriabine, Christine Brendel.
  The Presidency.
  (Know your government)
  Bibliography: p.
  Includes index.
  Summary: Surveys the history of the presidency, with
descriptions of its structure, current function, and
influence on American society.
  1. Presidents—United States—Juvenile literature.
[1. Presidents]   I. Title.   II. Series: Know your
government (New York, N.Y.)
JK517.S27   1988   353.03′1   87-23841
ISBN 1-55546-118-2
      0-7910-0872-X (pbk.)

CONTENTS

KNOW YOUR GOVERNMENT

CHELSEA HOUSE PUBLISHERS

INTRODUCTION

Government: Crises of Confidence

Arthur M. Schlesinger, jr.

From the start, Americans have regarded their government with a mixture of reliance and mistrust. The men who founded the republic did not doubt the indispensability of government. "If men were angels," observed the 51st Federalist Paper, "no government would be necessary." But men are not angels. Because human beings are subject to wicked as well as to noble impulses, government was deemed essential to assure freedom and order.

At the same time, the American revolutionaries knew that government could also become a source of injury and oppression. The men who gathered in Philadelphia in 1787 to write the Constitution therefore had two purposes in mind. They wanted to establish a strong central authority and to limit that central authority's capacity to abuse its power.

To prevent the abuse of power, the Founding Fathers wrote two basic principles into the new Constitution. The principle of federalism divided power between the state governments and the central authority. The principle of the separation of powers subdivided the central authority itself into three branches—the executive, the legislative, and the judiciary—so that "each may be a check on the other." The *Know Your Government* series focuses on the major executive departments and agencies in these branches of the federal government.

The Constitution did not plan the executive branch in any detail. After vesting the executive power in the president, it assumed the existence of "executive departments" without specifying what these departments should be. Congress began defining their functions in 1789 by creating the Departments of State, Treasury, and War. The secretaries in charge of these departments made up President Washington's first cabinet. Congress also provided for a legal officer, and President Washington soon invited the attorney general, as he was called, to attend cabinet meetings. As need required, Congress created more executive departments.

Setting up the cabinet was only the first step in organizing the American state. With almost no guidance from the Constitution, President Washington, seconded by Alexander Hamilton, his brilliant secretary of the treasury, equipped the infant republic with a working administrative structure. The Federalists believed in both executive energy and executive accountability and set high standards for public appointments. The Jeffersonian opposition had less faith in strong government and preferred local government to the central authority. But when Jefferson himself became president in 1801, although he set out to change the direction of policy, he found no reason to alter the framework the Federalists had erected.

By 1801 there were about 3,000 federal civilian employees in a nation of a little more than 5 million people. Growth in territory and population steadily enlarged national responsibilities. Thirty years later, when Jackson was president, there were more than 11,000 government workers in a nation of 13 million. The federal establishment was increasing at a faster rate than the population.

Jackson's presidency brought significant changes in the federal service. He believed that the executive branch contained too many officials who saw their jobs as "species of property" and as "a means of promoting individual interest." Against the idea of a permanent service based on life tenure, Jackson argued for the periodic redistribution of federal offices, contending that this was the democratic way and that official duties could be made "so plain and simple that men of intelligence may readily qualify themselves for their performance." He called this policy rotation-in-office. His opponents called it the spoils system.

In fact, partisan legend exaggerated the extent of Jackson's removals. More than 80 percent of federal officeholders retained their jobs. Jackson discharged no larger a proportion of government workers than Jefferson had done a generation earlier. But the rise in these years of mass political parties gave federal patronage new importance as a means of building the party and of rewarding activists. Jackson's successors were less restrained in the distribu-

8

tion of spoils. As the federal establishment grew—to nearly 40,000 by 1861—the politicization of the public service excited increasing concern.

After the Civil War the spoils system became a major political issue. High-minded men condemned it as the root of all political evil. The spoilsmen, said the British commentator James Bryce, "have distorted and depraved the mechanism of politics." Patronage, by giving jobs to unqualified, incompetent, and dishonest persons, lowered the standards of public service and nourished corrupt political machines. Office-seekers pursued presidents and cabinet secretaries without mercy. "Patronage," said Ulysses S. Grant after his presidency, "is the bane of the presidential office." "Every time I appoint someone to office," said another political leader, "I make a hundred enemies and one ingrate." George William Curtis, the president of the National Civil Service Reform League, summed up the indictment. He said,

> The theory which perverts public trusts into party spoils, making public
> employment dependent upon personal favor and not on proved merit,
> necessarily ruins the self-respect of public employees, destroys the
> function of party in a republic, prostitutes elections into a desperate
> strife for personal profit, and degrades the national character by lower-
> ing the moral tone and standard of the country.

The object of civil service reform was to promote efficiency and honesty in the public service and to bring about the ethical regeneration of public life. Over bitter opposition from politicians, the reformers in 1883 passed the Pendleton Act, establishing a bipartisan Civil Service Commission, competitive examinations, and appointment on merit. The Pendleton Act also gave the president authority to extend by executive order the number of "classified" jobs—that is, jobs subject to the merit system. The act applied initially only to about 14,000 of the more than 100,000 federal positions. But by the end of the 19th century 40 percent of federal jobs had moved into the classified category.

Civil service reform was in part a response to the growing complexity of American life. As society grew more organized and problems more technical, official duties were no longer so plain and simple that any person of intelligence could perform them. In public service, as in other areas, the all-round man was yielding ground to the expert, the amateur to the professional. The excesses of the spoils system thus provoked the counter-ideal of scientific public administration, separate from politics and, as far as possible, insulated against it.

The cult of the expert, however, had its own excesses. The idea that administration could be divorced from policy was an illusion. And in the realm of policy, the expert, however much segregated from partisan politics, can

9

never attain perfect objectivity. He remains the prisoner of his own set of values. It is these values rather than technical expertise that determine fundamental judgments of public policy. To turn over such judgments to experts, moreover, would be to abandon democracy itself; for in a democracy final decisions must be made by the people and their elected representatives. "The business of the expert," the British political scientist Harold Laski rightly said, "is to be on tap and not on top."

Politics, however, were deeply ingrained in American folkways. This meant intermittent tension between the presidential government, elected every four years by the people, and the permanent government, which saw presidents come and go while it went on forever. Sometimes the permanent government knew better than its political masters; sometimes it opposed or sabotaged valuable new initiatives. In the end a strong president with effective cabinet secretaries could make the permanent government responsive to presidential purpose, but it was often an exasperating struggle.

The struggle within the executive branch was less important, however, than the growing impatience with bureaucracy in society as a whole. The 20th century saw a considerable expansion of the federal establishment. The Great Depression and the New Deal led the national government to take on a variety of new responsibilities. The New Deal extended the federal regulatory apparatus. By 1940, in a nation of 130 million people, the number of federal workers for the first time passed the 1 million mark. The Second World War brought federal civilian employment to 3.8 million in 1945. With peace, the federal establishment declined to around 2 million by 1950. Then growth resumed, reaching 2.8 million by the 1980s.

The New Deal years saw rising criticism of "big government" and "bureaucracy." Businessmen resented federal regulation. Conservatives worried about the impact of paternalistic government on individual self-reliance, on community responsibility, and on economic and personal freedom. The nation in effect renewed the old debate between Hamilton and Jefferson in the early republic, although with an ironic exchange of positions. For the Hamiltonian constituency, the "rich and well-born," once the advocate of affirmative government, now condemned government intervention, while the Jeffersonian constituency, the plain people, once the advocate of a weak central government and of states' rights, now favored government intervention.

In the 1980s, with the presidency of Ronald Reagan, the debate has burst out with unusual intensity. According to conservatives, government intervention abridges liberty, stifles enterprise, and is inefficient, wasteful, and arbitrary. It disturbs the harmony of the self-adjusting market and creates worse troubles than it solves. Get government off our backs, according to the popular cliché, and our problems will solve themselves. When government is necessary, let it be at the local level, close to the people. Above all, stop the inexorable growth of the federal government.

In fact, for all the talk about the "swollen" and "bloated" bureaucracy, the federal establishment has not been growing as inexorably as many Americans seem to believe. In 1949, it consisted of 2.1 million people. Thirty years later, while the country had grown by 70 million, the federal force had grown only by 750,000. Federal workers were a smaller percentage of the population in 1985 than they were in 1955—or in 1940. The federal establishment, in short, has not kept pace with population growth. Moreover, national defense and the postal service account for 60 percent of federal employment.

Why then the widespread idea about the remorseless growth of government? It is partly because in the 1960s the national government assumed new and intrusive functions: affirmative action in civil rights, environmental protection, safety and health in the workplace, community organization, legal aid to the poor. Although this enlargement of the federal regulatory role was accompanied by marked growth in the size of government on all levels, the expansion has taken place primarily in state and local government. Whereas the federal force increased by only 27 percent in the 30 years after 1950, the state and local government force increased by an astonishing 212 percent.

Despite the statistics, the conviction flourishes in some minds that the national government is a steadily growing behemoth swallowing up the liberties of the people. The foes of Washington prefer local government, feeling it is closer to the people and therefore allegedly more responsive to popular needs. Obviously there is a great deal to be said for settling local questions locally. But local government is characteristically the government of the locally powerful. Historically, the way the locally powerless have won their human and constitutional rights has often been through appeal to the national government. The national government has vindicated racial justice against local bigotry, defended the Bill of Rights against local vigilantism, and protected natural resources against local greed. It has civilized industry and secured the rights of labor organizations. Had the states' rights creed prevailed, there would perhaps still be slavery in the United States.

The national authority, far from diminishing the individual, has given most Americans more personal dignity and liberty than ever before. The individual freedoms destroyed by the increase in national authority have been in the main the freedom to deny black Americans their rights as citizens; the freedom to put small children to work in mills and immigrants in sweatshops; the freedom to pay starvation wages, require barbarous working hours, and permit squalid working conditions; the freedom to deceive in the sale of goods and securities; the freedom to pollute the environment—all freedoms that, one supposes, a civilized nation can readily do without.

"Statements are made," said President John F. Kennedy in 1963, "labelling the Federal Government an outsider, an intruder, an adversary. . . . The United States Government is not a stranger or not an enemy. It is the people of fifty states joining in a national effort. . . . Only a great national effort by a great people working together can explore the mysteries of space, harvest the products at the bottom of the ocean, and mobilize the human, natural, and material resources of our lands."

So an old debate continues. However, Americans are of two minds. When pollsters ask large, spacious questions—Do you think government has become too involved in your lives? Do you think government should stop regulating business?—a sizable majority opposes big government. But when asked specific questions about the practical work of government—Do you favor social security? unemployment compensation? Medicare? health and safety standards in factories? environmental protection? government guarantee of jobs for everyone seeking employment? price and wage controls when inflation threatens?—a sizable majority approves of intervention.

In general, Americans do not want less government. What they want is more efficient government. They want government to do a better job. For a time in the 1970s, with Vietnam and Watergate, Americans lost confidence in the national government. In 1964, more than three-quarters of those polled had thought the national government could be trusted to do right most of the time. By 1980 only one-quarter was prepared to offer such trust. But by 1984 trust in the federal government to manage national affairs had climbed back to 45 percent.

Bureaucracy is a term of abuse. But it is impossible to run any large organization, whether public or private, without a bureaucracy's division of labor and hierarchy of authority. And we live in a world of large organizations. Without bureaucracy modern society would collapse. The problem is not to abolish bureaucracy, but to make it flexible, efficient, and capable of innovation.

Two hundred years after the drafting of the Constitution, Americans still regard government with a mixture of reliance and mistrust—a good combination. Mistrust is the best way to keep government reliable. Informed criticism

12

is the means of correcting governmental inefficiency, incompetence, and arbitrariness; that is, of best enabling government to play its essential role. For without government, we cannot attain the goals of the Founding Fathers. Without an understanding of government, we cannot have the informed criticism that makes government do the job right. It is the duty of every American citizen to know our government—which is what this series is all about.

The Oval Office in the White House is the president's formal workplace. Here, the chief executive makes decisions that profoundly affect the nation.

ONE

Inside the Oval Office

American political culture revolves around the actions of one person: the president of the United States. The president elicits many of the hopes, fears, and frustrations the American people express about their government. For most citizens, the person in the Oval Office embodies the laws, ideals, and strengths of the nation. Every day, thousands of people call or write to the White House to express their views on the chief executive's latest action or comment. They expect him to solve national crises, accept blame for national mistakes, and provide a sense of national purpose.

Because the president leads the strongest and wealthiest nation on earth and because he holds the key to the United States's atomic arsenal, citizens of other nations also focus a great deal of attention on him. As a result, almost every schoolchild in the world knows his name and what he looks like. And for many foreigners, the decisions made in the White House are often more important than those made by their own leaders.

The president boasts vast powers along with his tremendous fame. The Constitution outlined some of these powers when it established the presidency in 1787. Other powers have evolved during the past two centuries in response to national crises, changing international politics, and the personalities of those who have held the office. In modern times, no other head of state dominates

The president serves as the nation's chief diplomat. Here, Richard M. Nixon (left) and his wife visit the Great Wall during a 1972 visit to China.

so many different areas of government. The president of the United States is at once chief diplomat, supreme military commander, highest executive officer, a key instigator of legislation, and the leader of his party.

Although the president's powers have expanded considerably since the nation's early years, not every president has been able to exercise those powers. The amount of authority each chief executive commands depends on a variety of factors—for example, how well he communicates with the electorate, how smoothly he manages his staff, and how broadly he interprets the Constitution's definition of his office. It also depends to a certain degree on circumstances. Many of the presidents thought by historians to have been particularly effective, such as Abraham Lincoln, Woodrow Wilson, and Franklin D. Roosevelt, had the advantage of serving during periods of crisis, when their countrymen were willing to allow single individuals far-reaching powers. Probably the most important factor in determining how much power a president wields is how well he gets along with Congress. Under the Constitution's system of checks and balances, lawmakers have a mandate to restrict the chief executive's actions. A president who has Congress's support can effect substantial change, as Lyndon B. Johnson did when he orchestrated the major civil rights legislation of the 1960s. But a president who is faced with a Congress dominated by the rival political party will find it difficult to accomplish his party's goals.

As the president's powers have increased, so, too, have the difficulties of his position. He confronts such awesome tasks as managing the world's largest economy and setting the government's course in alleviating social injustice. America's status as a global power also requires him to monitor the country's relations with other nations and to keep a vigilant watch over developing crises on every continent. In the age of atomic weapons, even a small mistake in foreign relations could threaten world peace and possibly destroy civilization. In order to make responsible decisions about these complex issues, he must absorb an overwhelming amount of information.

Truly the presidency is a grueling job—the hours are long, the pressure is constant, criticism is inevitable. Even in less complex times, holders of the office lamented over the difficulty of their responsibilities. In September 1899, only two years after taking office, William McKinley said of the presidency, "I have had enough of it, heaven knows. I have had responsibilities enough to kill any man." Said Harry S. Truman after finishing his last term, "There is no exaltation in the office of the President of the United States—sorrow is the proper word." Yet politicians continue to aspire to the office. Perhaps they do so for the same reason Theodore Roosevelt so enjoyed his eight years in office: "It is fine to feel one's hand guiding great machinery."

A huge staff helps the president perform his myriad duties. The executive branch includes the president's personal staff, the Executive Office of the President, the cabinet, and numerous departments and bureaus. The distribution of power within the executive branch varies widely from one administration to the next. So does the extent to which each president allows his advisers access to the Oval Office. Some presidents, such as Franklin D. Roosevelt, have favored a "hands-on" management style, actively involving themselves in foreign and domestic policy. Other presidents, such as Ronald Reagan, have preferred to give their aides a great deal of autonomy in initiating policy. Ultimately, however, every president bears final responsibility for actions undertaken by his administration. For as Harry Truman once noted of the presidency, "The buck stops here."

Colonial soldiers confront the British in the Battle of Long Island, during the revolutionary war. Frustration with tyrannical British rule fueled the colonists' fight to establish a new government.

TWO

The Birth of the Presidency

In creating the office of the president of the United States, the framers of the Constitution were profoundly influenced by their experience with another form of executive power—the British monarchy. The king claimed to rule by "divine right," the belief that his authority was sanctioned by God.

Because the king lived in England, thousands of miles from America, he appointed governors to administer his colonies. These royal representatives allowed the colonists little say in how they were governed. They had power to appoint all judicial and law enforcement personnel and to veto acts passed by the colonial legislatures. To justify their despotic policies, the governors claimed to have prerogative power—sacred authority passed to them through the king. They used this power to enforce laws passed by the British Parliament, a legislative body in which the colonists had no representation. At first, colonists were reluctant to challenge an authority that they believed had been granted by God, although many resented the governors' power. But, as Parliament passed a series of harsh tax measures, the colonists began to question prerogative power. Gradually, they came to believe that such divine authority was vested not in the monarch and his representatives, but in the people themselves. So they began pressuring the British to limit the governors' power. The British, however, did not respond to these demands.

England's king George III claimed he had a "divine right" to rule his subjects. The colonists' experience with the British monarchy made them reluctant to vest all executive power in one person.

Meanwhile, tensions between the colonists and the British escalated. The colonists became increasingly frustrated with rule by a government in which they were not represented, and England's king George III grew impatient with their signs of rebelliousness. Tensions peaked in April 1775, when skirmishes broke out between British troops and colonial militias at Lexington and Concord, Massachusetts, sparking the revolutionary war.

At the beginning of the American Revolution, many colonists remained loyal to the king. But, as the war intensified, so did colonial opposition to the British government. Some of the most respected men in America—James Madison, Patrick Henry, and Thomas Jefferson—urged their compatriots to use the war not simply to seek greater influence in the British government but to strive for complete independence. Many spoke out against the very concept of monarchy. In 1776, Thomas Paine, a former cabinetmaker who had recently arrived in the colonies from Britain, decried kingship in his famous pamphlet, *Common Sense.* "These are the times that try men's souls," Paine wrote. "Government by kings was introduced into the world by heathens." The document sold more than 120,000 copies in fewer than 3 months. After the war, its stinging critique of the monarchy remained fixed in the minds of America's leaders as they considered the task of creating a new government.

The Articles of Confederation

After the British army surrendered in 1781, America's foremost revolutionary leaders convened in Philadelphia to create a set of laws to govern the new nation. They ratified the Articles of Confederation, the country's first national governing document and predecessor of the U.S. Constitution.

One of the most hotly debated points during the convention was the question of how executive power should be distributed. The experience delegates had with the British monarchy made many of them reluctant to vest executive authority in a single person. A chief executive, they reasoned, might take

The Articles of Confederation, ratified in 1781, established the nation's first government as an assembled body of state representatives.

ARTICLES

Of Confederation and perpetual Union between the States of *New-Hampshire, Massachusetts-Bay, Rhode-Island* and *Providence Plantations, Connecticut, New-York, New-Jersey, Pennsylvania, Delaware, Maryland, Virginia, North-Carolina, South-Carolina* and *Georgia.*

ARTICLE I. THE ſtile of this confederacy ſhall be "The United States of America."

Stile of the Confederacy

ART. II. EACH ſtate retains its ſovereignty, freedom and independence, and every power, juriſdiction and right, which is not by this confederation expreſly delegated to the United States, in Congreſs aſſembled.

Sovereignty and Independence of the reſpective States.

ART. III. THE ſaid ſtates hereby ſeverally enter into a firm league of friendſhip with each other, for their common defence, the ſecurity of their liberties, and their mutual and general welfare, binding themſelves to aſſiſt each other, againſt all force offered to, or attacks made upon them, or any of them, on account of religion, ſovereignty, trade, or any other pretence whatever.

Deſign of the Confederation, as it regards common ſecurity.

ART. IV. THE better to ſecure and perpetuate mutual friendſhip and intercourſe among the people of the different ſtates in this union, the free inhabitants of each of theſe ſtates, paupers, vagabonds, and fugitives from juſtice excepted, ſhall be entitled to all privileges and immunities of free citizens in the ſeveral ſtates ; and the people of each ſtate ſhall have free ingreſs and regreſs to and from any other ſtate, and ſhall enjoy therein all the privileges of trade and commerce, ſubject to the ſame duties, impoſitions and reſtrictions as the inhabitants thereof reſpectively, provided that ſuch reſtriction ſhall not extend ſo far as to prevent the removal of property imported into any ſtate, to any other ſtate of which the owner is an inhabitant ; provided alſo that no impoſition, duties or reſtriction ſhall be laid by any ſtate, on the property of the united ſtates, or either of them.

Social and mutual intercourſe among the States.

An 18th-century coin minted by Massachusetts. The Articles of Confederation prevented Congress from establishing a national currency; instead, each state minted its own coins.

advantage of his position to seize autocratic control. Ultimately, they decided that the country should have no executive branch at all. Instead, the Articles of Confederation named "the united states in congress assembled"—a group composed of representatives from each state—as the nation's sole governing body. This action placed all executive, legislative, and judicial functions of government in one body.

The decision not to establish a chief executive also reflected the delegates' desire to keep the federal government relatively weak in comparison to state administrations. In the new political system, states had authority in many more areas than Congress did. Each state could mint its own money, enter into its own trade treaties, and even declare war if it encountered "danger so imminent" that its leaders could not wait to consult Congress.

This arrangement prevented the federal government from becoming a tyrannical body, but it also led to administrative chaos, conflict among the states, and economic instability. The variance of laws from state to state caused endless confusion in conducting interstate trade. The relative weakness of the federal government kept people from developing a sense of loyalty to the nation as a whole, from "thinking continentally," in Alexander Hamilton's words. State representatives to Congress fought without hesitation for local goals, sharply dividing the various delegations to the legislative body. Even when members of Congress agreed, the Articles of Confederation gave them little power to act. They prohibited Congress from collecting taxes, establishing a national currency, and regulating trade. Congress's lack of authority in economic matters left it powerless to remedy the severe depression that ensued when the British Commonwealth—America's primary trading partner before the revolutionary war—enacted a boycott on American goods. Meanwhile, economic policies pursued by the states caused extreme hardship for farmers. High state taxes ate up most of each farmer's income, while skyrocketing inflation, brought on by the issuance of a separate currency in each state, undermined the value of farmland.

As conditions worsened, many of the founding fathers became convinced that the federal government had to be strengthened in order to effect an economic recovery. In 1786, James Madison called for a national convention to reorganize the government. At first, several states refused to participate. Then, toward the end of the year, farmers in western Massachusetts, led by revolutionary war captain Daniel Shays, staged a six-month rebellion to protest their state's harsh economic policies. The rebels used force to prevent western Massachusetts courts from convening. Similar uprisings followed in other parts of the country. Worried that the unrest would continue to spread, leaders from every state agreed to attend the national convention.

Massachusetts farmers cheer as a supporter of Shays's Rebellion brawls with an opponent. This 1786 protest against harsh economic policies convinced state representatives to reexamine the Articles of Confederation.

The Constitutional Convention

In the spring of 1787, the country's most respected and learned leaders convened in Philadelphia to reexamine the Articles of Confederation. By the time they adjourned in September, they had created an entirely new governing document—the Constitution. The 55 delegates included most of the men who had led the Revolution—James Madison, Alexander Hamilton, and Benjamin Franklin, among others. George Washington served as the convention's chairman.

These men faced an enormous task: creating a set of laws to unify and preserve the entire nation. Hundreds of problems needed solutions. On the issue of executive power, the delegates' views had changed markedly since the creation of the Articles of Confederation. Their experience seemed to demonstrate that without a chief executive, the government lacked sufficient authority to guarantee domestic peace, to improve economic conditions, and to establish ties with foreign nations. The problem now was to reconcile their desire for individual leadership with their fear that a monarchy would develop.

For guidance in solving this problem, the delegates consulted the works of the most influential political philosophers of their time—John Locke, William

Political philosopher John Locke believed that power should be distributed equally among several branches of government. State representatives adopted this principle in writing the Constitution.

James Madison worked with other delegates to the Constitutional Convention to develop the "Virginia Plan," which established the executive branch and outlined its powers and limitations.

Blackstone, and Baron Charles de Montesquieu. These writers provided a general model for the new government. They argued that the way to preserve an ideal democracy was to divide authority equally among several branches of government and to give each branch various means—called "checks and balances"—by which to restrict the powers of the others. Accepting this general principle, the delegates established three branches of government: legislative, judicial, and executive.

In fashioning the new executive branch, the delegates were influenced by the example of the New York state government, in which the chief executive, the governor, had proved especially effective. The governor of New York, unlike most other state governors, had considerable powers. His term was relatively long (three years). He was commander in chief of the state's military forces. He had authority to convene the legislature, recommend bills for the lawmakers' consideration, and execute the laws they passed.

The personality of George Washington also played an important part in determining the shape of the presidency. Most of the delegates agreed from the beginning that Washington would be the first president. Because most of the delegates trusted him implicitly, they were willing to give the office more power than they would have otherwise. As South Carolina delegate Pierce

George Washington presides over the Constitutional Convention of 1787. Because the delegates trusted Washington, they gave the presidency more power than they otherwise would have.

Butler later observed, the office they created would have been a much weaker one "had not many of the members cast their eyes toward General Washington as President, and shaped their ideas of the Powers to be given as President, by their opinions of his virtue."

The office of the presidency was further molded in constitutional debates. During the course of the convention, state delegations proposed various plans for organizing the presidency. The Virginia Plan eventually served as the model for the constitutional definition of the presidency.

Designed by Madison and the other Virginia delegates, the Virginia Plan called for an unspecified number of executive officers to be elected to a single term by the national legislature. It granted this executive branch a guaranteed salary, the general authority to execute national laws, and the power to veto legislation. The plan also granted Congress the right to impeach (formally charge) executive officers for malpractice or neglect of duty.

Although the delegates unanimously accepted most of the Virginia Plan's general provisions, they disagreed about its specific proposals on how the president should be elected, how long each presidential term should be, and the maximum number of terms a president should be allowed to serve. Unable to decide how the presidency should be organized, the delegates passed the question on to the Committee on Postponed Matters, which met on the matter in August 1787. The delegates voted to approve the committee's suggestions and incorporated them into the final draft of the Constitution.

On September 17, 1787, the committee presented the printed version of the Constitution of the United States of America to the delegates for their signatures. The final result of the debate on the presidency was Article II, outlining the privileges of and limitations on the nation's chief executive. Later amendments—the Twelfth, Twentieth, and Twenty-fifth—would further detail the president's powers and duties.

The Constitutional Presidency

Article II of the Constitution has four sections that define the qualifications, duties, and powers of the nation's chief executive. The first section describes the criteria for a presidential candidate. This person must be a natural-born citizen of the United States who has reached age 35 and has resided in this country for at least 14 years. (Because many of the Constitution's framers were not born in the United States, they included an exception to this rule: A person who was not a natural-born citizen but was a citizen when the Constitution was adopted could also become president. This clause was never tested, however, and soon became obsolete.)

Section 1 also provides rules for presidential elections. Although Americans now have the right to vote for their president, that right is not granted by the Constitution. (Election by popular vote evolved in the 19th century in response to changes in society.) Instead, the Constitution provides for the electoral system that was used during the nation's early years. Under the system, small groups of representatives from each state legislature, called "electors," gathered in their respective states to cast ballots for the presidency. The number of electors allotted to each state was determined by population, equaling the number of federal senators and congressmen from that state.

Each elector was to cast two ballots: one for his first choice for president and the other for his second choice. One of the ballots had to be cast for a candidate from a state other than the elector's own. The person who received the most electoral votes was declared president, and the person with the second largest number of votes became vice-president. The Twelfth Amendment later altered this system by instructing each elector to cast one vote for president and one for vice-president.

The third part of Section 1 discusses presidential succession. It stipulates that if the chief executive dies, resigns, or becomes unable to discharge his duties, the vice-president assumes his duties. This provision does not state, however, that the vice-president acquires the title of president, merely that he assumes the president's responsibilities. In 1933, Congress ratified the Twentieth Amendment, which specifies that a vice-president-elect (one who has not yet taken office) becomes president upon the death of a president-elect. Not until Congress passed the Twenty-fifth Amendment in 1967 did the Constitution state that the vice-president becomes president in case the chief executive is removed from office for any reason.

In its final two clauses, Section 1 describes the presidential salary—stipulating that the president's pay may neither decrease nor increase during his term in office—and establishes the oath of office that each president must recite on inauguration day: "I do solemnly swear (or affirm) that I will faithfully execute the office of President of the United States, and will to the best of my ability, preserve, protect and defend the Constitution of the United States."

Article II's second section outlines the president's powers. First, it establishes the president as commander in chief of the nation's armed services and "the militia of the several States." It empowers the president to request

The House Judiciary Committee holds a 1974 hearing to consider impeaching Richard M. Nixon. The Constitution empowers Congress to remove the president from office if he abuses his position.

The chief executive serves as commander in chief of the nation's armed services. Here, Franklin D. Roosevelt (center) reviews a naval fleet in 1934.

periodic reports from each "principal officer" (heads of cabinet-level departments) and to pardon offenses against the United States, except in cases of impeachment. The Constitution's framers considered pardoning power (one of the powers held by British monarchs) an integral part of executive power.

Section 2 also gives the president the power to make treaties with foreign countries and, with the Senate's approval, appoint ambassadors, judges, and all government officials not otherwise provided for in the Constitution, including cabinet members and department heads. It adds that if an office becomes vacant when Congress is not in session, the president may make an appointment without its approval.

Section 3 deals primarily with the president's relationship with Congress. It requires the president to address Congress periodically about the "state of the Union," in order to keep lawmakers apprised of current administration policies. It gives him the right to recommend bills to Congress and even convene and adjourn both houses if "he shall think proper." Finally, Section 3 allows the president to receive ambassadors and public ministers, to commission officers, and to "take care that the laws shall be faithfully executed."

Although rarely used, Section 4 of Article II is vital to democracy. It empowers Congress to remove the president, vice-president, or any other civil official if he is impeached for—and convicted of—treason, bribery, or any other "high crimes and misdemeanors." The Constitution's framers included this clause so that the legislature could remove from office a president who abuses his position.

In 1787, the Constitution outlined presidential powers and duties, although it left many of the details unclear. Over the next 200 years, the exact nature and extent of the president's role was shaped by the nation's crises, the public's mood, and the convictions and personalities of the men who held the office.

George Washington takes the oath of office during his inaugural ceremony on April 30, 1789. Washington was a strong leader who established many presidential powers that exist today.

THREE

The Evolution of
Presidential Power

In 1789, the nation's electors unanimously selected George Washington as the first president of the United States. Washington, however, took office reluctantly. He understood the immense responsibilities he would have to shoulder as the new nation's first president. "The first transactions of a nation . . . make the deepest impression," he wrote before his inauguration. He was right. More than any man who has held the office, Washington helped define the shape of the presidency.

Washington broadly interpreted the constitutional definition of his office. He believed that his authority extended beyond responsibilities specifically mentioned in Section 2 to include what he called "implied powers." Among these powers, he argued, was the right to help create new governmental institutions, as long as the new bodies were not expressly prohibited by the Constitution and as long as their establishment helped achieve constitutional goals. Operating under these assumptions, Washington set up a national bank, even though, as James Madison pointed out, delegates to the Constitutional Convention had rejected a clause authorizing the government to issue corporate charters. Creating the bank was permissible, Washington argued, because it would achieve the constitutional goal of "prosperity."

Washington (right) meets with members of his first cabinet. His conferences with chief advisers established a tradition that later presidents followed by scheduling regular cabinet meetings.

The energetic and charismatic leader initiated many other programs during his two terms in office. Under his administration, a national currency was issued, tariffs were enacted to encourage trade, patent and copyright laws were passed, and the army and navy were reorganized.

Many of the new programs Washington introduced had to be approved by Congress. In getting them approved, Washington played a much more active role in the legislative process than the framers of the Constitution had envisioned. Although the framers had given the president power to "recommend legislation," they expected Congress to be the main source of new bills. But during Washington's terms, the majority of legislation that was passed by Congress was initially conceived and written by the president and his staff.

Washington's greatest impact on the presidency was in the field of foreign policy. Although the Constitution had delegated the chief executive a fair amount of authority to establish foreign policy, it did not specify how the president was to exercise his power. For example, the Constitution had made the president responsible for entertaining foreign envoys, but it had not specified which branch of government should decide which representatives he was to meet. By arrogating this latter power to himself, Washington acquired the right to determine which nations would be America's allies. He also established treaty negotiation as the chief executive's exclusive province by refusing Congress's demands that he release documents relating to the negotiation of the Jay Treaty, a pact with Britain. In 1793, he further extended presidential powers in foreign policy by issuing—without congressional approval—the Proclamation of Neutrality, which declared that the United States and its citizens would not involve themselves in foreign disputes.

Washington also created many presidential traditions. For example, his regular meetings with his chief advisers—including the heads of the State, War, and Treasury departments—were forerunners of presidential cabinet meetings. His decision not to run for office in 1796 established the tradition of presidents serving no more than two terms, a custom that subsequent presidents maintained until Franklin D. Roosevelt ran for a third term in 1940. (Roosevelt's election to four consecutive terms of office led to the passage of the Twenty-second Amendment, which restricted the number of terms a president could serve to two.)

When Washington left office in 1796, after serving two terms, he left the presidency far stronger than most of the Constitution's framers had imagined was possible. Although some Americans worried that the presidency had become too powerful, Washington's authority had helped build respect for the executive office—and the new nation.

Elections and Party Politics

The 1796 presidential race tested the Constitution's election rules for the first time. (The rules had been unimportant in the first two campaigns because Washington had run unopposed.) Two bitter political enemies—John Adams and Thomas Jefferson—vied for election as the nation's second president.

33

The President's Lady

If the presidency is America's toughest job, then the role of first lady is quite possibly the second toughest. What makes the position especially difficult is that its duties and responsibilities are not clearly defined. Martha Washington chose to concentrate on hosting receptions and dinners and providing domestic support for her husband. Her successor, Abigail Adams, showed such an avid interest in government policy that many referred to her as "Mrs. President." Dolley Madison, the third woman to occupy the position, won the hearts of the American people with her ebullient personality. Since that time most first ladies have adopted one of these three basic roles: hostess, unofficial political adviser, or celebrity.

During the 19th century, first ladies attracted minimal press coverage and inspired little popular interest. There were, however, notable exceptions. Among them was Frances Folsom, who at age 21 became engaged to marry Grover Cleveland during his first term of office. Her youth and beauty fired the public's interest. Whenever Cleveland appeared in public during their engagement, bands played a wedding march; one creative conductor had his band play the Gilbert and Sullivan song "He's Going to Marry Yum-Yum." Their marriage boosted Cleveland's political popularity.

But not all first ladies were treated as kindly. Mary Lincoln, who suffered from severe emotional problems during her husband's presidency, was fiercely attacked by the newspapers. One sympathetic reporter wrote in 1861, "If Mrs. Lincoln were a prize fighter, a foreign danseuse, or a condemned convict on the way to execution, she could not be treated more indecently than she is by a portion of the New York press."

During the 20th century, first ladies became increasingly visible. They also began to exert greater influence over national affairs. Woodrow Wilson's second wife, Edith Bolling Wilson, was perhaps the most powerful of all first ladies. After her husband suffered a debilitating stroke in late 1919, she decided which officials and which papers he could see, convinced him not to resign, and made sure the public did not discover the seriousness of his condition. Many historians have described her as a "president-in-fact."

Edith Bolling Wilson helps her husband, President Woodrow Wilson, sign a document.

Onlookers watch as Lady Bird Johnson plants a fir tree in Texas's Big Bend National Park in 1966.

But the woman who made the position of first lady an independent political force was Eleanor Roosevelt. She traveled the country on fact-finding missions for her husband, whose physical handicap limited his mobility. She held her own press conferences—to which only women reporters were invited. And in 1935, she began to publish a daily newspaper column entitled "My Day." She understood, as one reporter put it, that "American people must make a carnival around their First Lady," and decided to use their interest in her to focus attention on social causes—particularly world peace, civil rights, and the plight of the poor.

Bess Truman and Mamie Eisenhower, the two first ladies who immediately followed Eleanor Roosevelt, were much less active than their dynamic predecessor. But the first lady returned to the limelight when Jacqueline Kennedy moved into the White House in 1961. Mrs. Kennedy, at 31 the youngest first lady since Frances Folsom Cleveland, captured the attention not only of Americans but of the world. While her beauty and intelligence enhanced her husband's youthful image, her style changed the look of American fashion. Her main substantive project was restoring the White House in the manner of the 19th century, rescuing from the White House basement such antiques as Monroe's flatware and Lincoln's china. Though uninterested in politics, she lent sophistication to the Kennedy administration.

With the exception of Patricia Nixon, who remained aloof from both politics and the news media, the first ladies who followed Mrs. Kennedy used their position to advance special projects. Lady Bird Johnson sought the "beautification" of America, leading a campaign to plant flowers and shrubs around the Washington area, helping to secure the passage of the Highway Beautification Act, and supporting the ecology movement. Betty Ford championed women's rights, drawing particular attention because her views were more liberal than her husband's. Rosalynn Carter, who was the first wife of a president to attend cabinet meetings, concentrated on seeking better treatment for the elderly and the mentally ill. And Nancy Reagan focused her efforts on heightening public awareness about the dangers of drug abuse.

Clearly, the position of first lady allows ample room for individuality. The women who have held the position have helped define its role in American political culture, just as their husbands have helped shape the presidency.

The tense 1796 presidential race between John Adams (left) and Thomas Jefferson (right) tested national election laws for the first time and ultimately revealed flaws.

Adams belonged to the Federalist party, whose members supported a strong federal government and favored England in foreign affairs; Jefferson represented the rival party, the Democratic-Republicans, whose members favored France and believed that political power should be centered in state governments.

The results of the 1796 election revealed a flaw in the electoral system. According to the Constitution, each elector was supposed to cast two votes for president, choosing from a field of candidates that included not only presidential hopefuls but also their vice-presidential running mates. Regardless of party affiliation, however, the person with the most votes became president and the person with the second-highest number of votes became vice-president. Thus it was possible for members of two different parties to serve as president and vice-president. In 1796, Adams received the most votes, but his running mate, Charles Pinckney, lost to Thomas Jefferson. Therefore, Adams became president and Jefferson—his archrival—became vice-president.

This arrangement made for a highly unstable administration. Federalist control of Congress enabled Adams to extend his authority by steering through legislation such as the Alien Act, which empowered the president to remove from the country any noncitizens he considered dangerous to national security. But Adams also used this power to deport certain Democratic-Republican opponents. At the same time, Jefferson served as a check on Adams's power. In a document called the Kentucky Resolution, Jefferson criticized the Alien Act as an unfair intrusion of the federal government into areas reserved by the Constitution for the states.

The framers of the Constitution had not created the electoral system with political parties in mind. In fact, many of them believed that they had constructed a system that would discourage the creation of parties or factions. But the 1796 election and the Adams administration demonstrated that American politicians were clearly divided into two distinct camps. The 1796 election also began the tradition of aggressive campaigning. The Democratic-Republicans widely distributed campaign literature that portrayed Jefferson as the representative of the people and Adams as a puppet of monied interests. In turn, the Federalists attacked Jefferson as an enemy of the union, a tool of France, and an unrealistic philosopher unfit to lead the nation. For his part, Jefferson remained aloof from this factionalism. "If I could not go to heaven but with a party," he said, "I would not go there at all." But by 1800, when Jefferson again challenged an opponent for the presidency, he plunged wholeheartedly into the fray.

The flaw in the electoral system that marred the 1796 election surfaced again in the 1800 presidential election. The electors wanted Jefferson for president and his running mate Aaron Burr for vice-president. But the election was a tie, and according to the Constitution, Congress had to choose a winner. For 35 agonizing roll calls, the election remained deadlocked as Burr's supporters in the House blocked Jefferson's election. A mob of Jefferson supporters took up positions at all entrances to the House chambers, insisting that they would not allow Burr to steal the election. Finally, on the 36th roll call, lawmakers chose Jefferson as president. But the confusion caused by these elections spurred Congress to pass the Twelfth Amendment in 1804. It stipulated that electors

Aaron Burr, shown here, won the same number of votes as Thomas Jefferson in the 1800 presidential election, but he lost the presidency when Congress declared Jefferson the winner.

must cast two separate ballots—one vote for president and the other vote for vice-president.

As Adams did, Jefferson used the presidency to advance party goals, continuing a tradition that has been part of the American presidency ever since. Jefferson was the first president to lead his political party while in office. He also used his party affiliations to sway fellow Democratic-Republicans in Congress. To strengthen his party's political influence and to give it greater unity, Jefferson made government appointments on the basis of political patronage—a practice known as the "spoils" system. He rewarded political supporters and fellow party members with ambassadorships, secretaryships, and other government jobs to ensure that he had the support of his highest officers.

The Quiet Revolution

Jefferson left office when his second term ended in 1809. The next three presidents, James Madison (1809–1817), James Monroe (1817–1825), and John Quincy Adams (1825–1829), modified the presidency very little. But while they held the office, a "quiet revolution" subtly transformed the American perception of the presidency and forever changed the way the nation chose its leaders. The original Constitution did not provide for popular elections, largely because many delegates believed that the public could not understand the complex issues involved in selecting a leader. For similar reasons, most states also did not hold popular elections.

During the first two decades of the 19th century, however, changes in the American way of life began to alter public political attitudes. As the country expanded westward and new states entered the Union, new economic opportunities arose for poor and uneducated people. Along with these economic changes came a change in the political climate. Americans from all walks of life soon demanded a share of the political power formerly reserved for the wealthy and well educated.

These demands changed election procedures. Between 1790 and 1824, most states eliminated laws tying the right to vote to property ownership or tax payments. In addition, the parties changed the way they selected their presidential candidates, giving the public greater influence. By 1824 traditional caucuses, in which presidential candidates were chosen secretly by state congressional committees, were replaced by national nominating conventions, in which party representatives from each state met openly to choose candidates.

Technological changes, such as the development of the steamboat and the

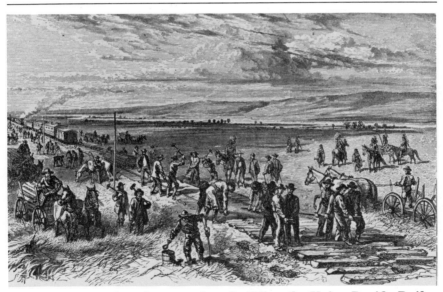

This 1867 engraving shows workers building the Union Pacific Railroad. Transportation advances gave Americans greater mobility and exposed them to national, rather than regional, concerns.

With his hand on the Bible, Andrew Jackson (left) takes the oath of office in 1829. Jackson defied Congress during his presidency and caused legislators to exert tighter control over his successors.

steam locomotive, also contributed to the popularization of American politics. As transportation improved, people in the country's most remote areas suddenly gained access to news about national events. As more people obtained the vote and as more Americans became informed about national news, the nature of political campaigns changed dramatically. For the first time, candidates for the presidency had to campaign actively among the people. They began holding parades and barbecues and producing political campaign buttons, china, and novelties to gain public support.

"Let the People Rule"

Andrew Jackson, who was elected to the presidency in 1828, was the first to benefit from the changes in the electoral process. An uneducated pioneer from Tennessee, Jackson was the first man born to a poor family to occupy the presidency. Elected by a large majority with the slogan "Let the people rule," Jackson strongly believed that he represented all the nation's people. Convinced that he had a mandate to govern, this extremely active president did not hesitate to defy the other branches of government and to push legislation he thought the people supported.

Jackson dominated Congress, using his executive veto power to block legislation he disliked. (Previous presidents had vetoed only legislation they considered unconstitutional.) He also expanded the political patronage system. To increase Jackson's popularity, his supporters founded national newspapers to present his point of view. He was reelected in 1832.

Jackson's strong presidency made it difficult for those who followed him to match his power. In effect, he weakened the presidency for his immediate successors by causing Congress to exercise tighter control over the executive branch. Congress stifled the moves of President Martin Van Buren, who was elected in 1836. When Van Buren ran for reelection in 1840 he lost to William Henry Harrison.

Death of a President

Harrison's term, the shortest in the nation's history, created another crisis for the American presidency. In 1841, Harrison died after only one month in office. Article II, Section 1 of the Constitution states that in case of the president's death or removal from office, his duties "shall devolve on the Vice President."

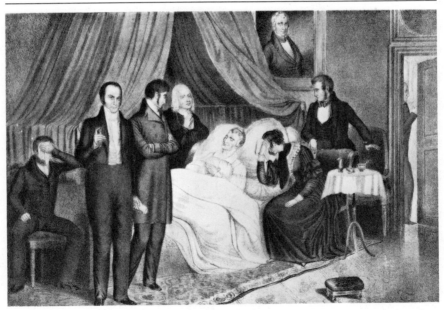

William Henry Harrison's death in 1841, after only one month in office, left the presidency vacant and forced Congress to decide whether the vice-president had the right to assume the title of president.

41

Nowhere does it state, however, that the vice-president has the right to assume the title of president. Nonetheless, after Harrison's death, Vice-president John Tyler boldly took his title.

Some members of Congress objected to Tyler becoming president. They argued that Tyler should be "acting president" until another president could be elected. Eventually, however, Congress accepted Tyler as president, starting a new tradition. Since then, vice-presidents have assumed the duties and the title of president when presidents have died. This tradition did not become law, however, until Congress ratified the Twenty-fifth Amendment in 1967.

Tyler was succeeded by James K. Polk (1845–1849), the first "dark horse" to run for office. (The term *dark horse*, which refers to a political candidate who is unexpectedly nominated, originated in the world of horse racing, where it refers to a horse whose racing prowess is unknown.) Polk entered the presidential race very late, when the Democratic party selected him as its candidate at its nominating convention. As president, Polk maintained many of Jackson's domestic policies and pursued an aggressive foreign policy. Although

Vice-president John Tyler assumed the duties and title of president after Harrison's death. After some objection, Congress accepted Tyler as president, starting a new tradition.

Abraham Lincoln (left) confers with General George B. McClellan during the Civil War. Lincoln exerted his authority independently of Congress and ultimately increased presidential powers.

not especially brilliant or charismatic, Polk accomplished a great deal during his single term in office—primarily because he had the support of Congress. Under his administration, the United States acquired more than 1 million square miles of new territory and extended its western boundary from the Mississippi River to the Pacific Ocean.

The presidents who followed Polk—Zachary Taylor (1849–1850), Millard Fillmore (1850–1853), Franklin Pierce (1853–1857), and James Buchanan (1857–1861)—faced powerful Congresses and made few lasting marks on the office. But the problems that led to the Civil War shattered the serenity of these presidencies. The Civil War threatened to destroy the Union but ultimately increased presidential powers.

Lincoln and the Civil War

The 1860 election sharply divided the nation. For years, political, economic, and social disputes between the North and the South had imperiled the Union. By 1860, many southern states threatened to leave the Union if the Republican party, which believed in strong federal control of the economy and the abolition of slavery, gained the presidency.

Southern threats became reality in November 1860, after Republican candidate Abraham Lincoln was elected president. Only one month after his

43

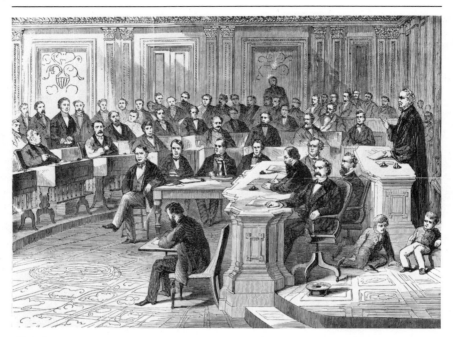

The Senate votes to impeach Andrew Johnson in 1868. Although the Senate failed to convict Johnson, Congress restricted the power of his immediate successors.

election, South Carolina seceded from the Union. Other southern states soon followed. By Lincoln's inauguration on March 4, 1861, seven states had seceded. One month later, southern troops fired on the U.S. Army garrison at Fort Sumter, South Carolina, and the Civil War began.

The pressing needs caused by the Civil War forced the new president to seize a great deal of power. Because Congress was not in session during the first few weeks of the war, Lincoln governed the country virtually on his own. Without consulting any other government branch, he added 41,000 men to the armed services, summoned volunteers and state militias into active duty, and released $2 million in federal funds for war supplies. He also closed the post office to "treasonable" correspondence, blockaded southern ports to hinder weapons shipments, and suspended the writ of *habeas corpus* (which protects citizens from unlawful imprisonment) in parts of the country.

Even after Congress convened, Lincoln continued to exert his authority independently of the rest of the government. His term in office illustrated that a president could assume tremendous authority during a national crisis.

Limiting Presidential Power

After Lincoln's assassination in 1865, Vice-president Andrew Johnson (1865–1869) assumed the presidency. Because Johnson inherited the position, he also inherited Lincoln's cabinet. Johnson believed that even though he had not been elected, he had the same right as other presidents to make appointments and dismiss staff members. But some members of Congress wanted to limit these actions, so in 1867 they passed the Tenure of Office Act, which prohibited the president from hiring or firing advisers without the Senate's approval.

Johnson felt that the power to remove advisers from office—exercised by every president since Washington—was an inherent right of the presidency. Therefore, he ignored the Tenure of Office Act and dismissed Secretary of War Edwin M. Stanton. The House of Representatives responded by exercising its constitutional power to impeach a president for "high crimes and misdemeanors."

The Senate failed to convict Johnson, and Stanton resigned from office. Although the outcome was a victory for Johnson, it ushered in a quarter-century of tighter congressional control of the executive branch. Congress severely limited the power of the presidents who followed Johnson. It did this

Ulysses S. Grant (left), shown here with his family, followed Johnson into office. His presidency ushered in an era of executive weakness that lasted 27 years.

This sample ballot from the 1892 election lists the names of all the candidates for various positions, regardless of their party affiliation, allowing voters to choose candidates from different parties.

by originating much of the nation's legislation during this period and by passing laws that gave Congress greater control over the federal budget.

Ulysses S. Grant (1869–1877), Rutherford B. Hayes (1877–1881), James Garfield (1881), Chester Allen Arthur (1881–1885), Grover Cleveland (1885–1889 and 1893–1897), and Benjamin Harrison (1889–1893) all saw their legislative agendas thwarted by Congress. Their presidencies were further weakened because the Tenure of Office Act limited their ability to control their presidential staffs, and no major crises arose that would have allowed them to seize power as Lincoln had during the Civil War. In addition, none of these men was particularly well qualified to serve as president. Each had won office primarily because, during this period, Americans tended to vote for parties, not individuals. In addition, electoral margins in this period were very slim. No president could believe that he had received a mandate at the polls.

This period of executive weakness ended in 1896, when Republican William McKinley won the presidency by a large margin of the popular vote.

McKinley's popularity and his party's majority in both houses of Congress enabled him to exercise his executive authority to a fuller extent than his immediate predecessors had.

The Australian Ballot

McKinley's large margin of victory was made possible by the widespread use of the Australian ballot, a secret ballot issued by the government and modeled after ballots used in Australia. By 1896, most states had adopted the Australian ballot. Before the new ballot came into use, a voter registered his selections on a ballot provided by the political party of his choice. This ballot listed only the names of the party's candidates for each open office, forcing voters to vote along rigid party lines. The Australian ballot, on the other hand, listed the names of all the candidates for various offices so that a voter could "split his ticket" (vote for candidates from different parties) if he desired. Officials from both parties distributed the new ballots at public polling places, where individuals could cast their votes in private booths. This system discouraged party officials from intimidating voters and prevented voters from casting more than one ballot each.

The Australian ballot diminished the power of the political parties. To regain their strength, parties redoubled their efforts to nominate strong, appealing candidates who would draw voters to the polls. The candidates Americans chose would guide the nation through its most trying period—the 20th century.

Theodore Roosevelt delivers a rousing speech to a group of labor supporters in 1902. Tremendous popular support enabled Roosevelt to pave the way for labor reforms in the 20th century.

FOUR

The Modern
Presidency

At the beginning of the 20th century, the United States experienced a wave of immigration and a dramatic rise in industrial output. These factors greatly increased the country's population, economic strength, and importance in world affairs. As advances in communications and transportation spanned the gaps between the United States and Europe, the presidency became an office of international significance.

Theodore Roosevelt led the nation into the new century. The popular Spanish-American-War hero took office after McKinley was assassinated in 1901 and proceeded to become one of the most innovative chief executives in history. In foreign affairs he used executive agreements, acts that do not require congressional approval, to conclude a series of treaties that gave the United States a high profile in international affairs. On the domestic front, Roosevelt used the visibility his office gave him to speak directly to the people. Turning the office into what he called a "bully pulpit," he gave the American public a sense of national purpose while successfully molding public opinion. Tremendous popular support gave him the leverage he needed to steer through Congress substantial legislation to foster conservation and to protect commerce from unlawful monopolies and business practices.

Roosevelt's successor, William Howard Taft, made few changes to the

A woman casts her ballot in the 1922 presidential election. Women won the right to vote when the Nineteenth Amendment to the Constitution was ratified in 1920.

presidency during his 1909–1913 term. But Woodrow Wilson, president from 1913–1921, significantly increased the power of the office. When the United States entered World War I in 1917, Wilson broadened governmental control of the economy. As Lincoln did, Wilson expanded presidential authority during a national crisis.

At the same time, the power of the electorate also grew. The Nineteenth Amendment, ratified in 1920, gave the vote, and thus political influence, to millions of American women. Labor unions and other organizations also began to exert political leverage. After Wilson left office in 1921, the power of the voters continued to increase, while presidential power declined during the administrations of Warren G. Harding (1921–1923), Calvin Coolidge (1923–1929), and Herbert Hoover (1929–1933). But Franklin D. Roosevelt, who became president in 1933, created one of the most powerful presidencies ever.

The Roosevelt Years

Roosevelt took office at the height of the Great Depression, the worst economic disaster in American history. The crisis atmosphere surrounding his first term in office allowed him to make bold moves. He transformed the nation's social and financial systems by introducing the New Deal, an enormous package of legislative reforms. His New Deal transformed the economy—and the government's role in it—by creating federal job programs and instituting welfare, social security, and a minimum wage.

This dynamic president also increased the government's size and power, especially in the executive branch. In 1939 he created the Executive Office of the President, adding dozens of new members to the White House staff. He appointed the first woman cabinet member, Secretary of Labor Frances Perkins, and established the vice-president's role as the president's emissary.

Roosevelt was the first president to speak to the public over the radio. Following the lead of his cousin, Theodore Roosevelt, he fostered popular support for his administration by charming the public in broadcasts known as "fireside chats." He also skillfully manipulated the press into presenting his viewpoints favorably.

A new crisis affected Roosevelt's administration in 1939, when World War II began in Europe. It allowed Roosevelt to increase presidential power even further by instituting such measures as the first peacetime draft and providing military assistance to Great Britain. After the Japanese bombed Pearl Harbor

Franklin D. Roosevelt used the power of radio to communicate courage and hope to millions of Americans throughout the Great Depression and World War II.

in 1941 and the United States entered the war, presidential power reached its peak. Congress passed the First and Second War Powers Acts, allowing Roosevelt to control the national economy through wage and price restraints and to abridge civil rights by jailing Japanese Americans in detention camps. As commander in chief of the United States armed forces, Roosevelt made military decisions that affected the lives of millions around the world, thus securing the president's role as a world leader.

Roosevelt's enormous power was made possible by his boldest break with tradition: He sought—and won—four terms as president. Although the Constitution did not stipulate the number of terms a president could serve, previous presidents had followed Washington's example by serving a maximum of two terms. The incredible power Roosevelt garnered in his four terms led Congress to pass the Twenty-second Amendment to the Constitution in 1951. This amendment officially limited presidents to two terms in office.

Farmers report for work on a federal water conservation program in 1936. During the Great Depression, Roosevelt urged Congress to provide funding for many federal work programs.

Japenese Americans crowd an internment camp during World War II. Presidential power reached a new high when Congress allowed Roosevelt to abridge civil rights by imprisoning American citizens.

The Cold War Begins

When Roosevelt died in 1945 at the beginning of his fourth term, Vice-president Harry S. Truman became president. Crises marked Truman's presidency and encouraged the further growth of presidential power. Entering office in the final days of World War II, Truman assumed the role of commander in chief and made the decision to drop atomic bombs on the Japanese cities of Hiroshima and Nagasaki.

After the war ended, the cold war (a conflict between the United States and the Soviet Union without military action) and the Korean War allowed Truman to continue exercising vast authority. He committed troops to Korea without congressional approval, setting the stage for later administrations' involvement in Southeast Asia. In addition, he increased his staff and created new agencies and offices, such as the Central Intelligence Agency (CIA) and the National

Roosevelt (left) confers with British prime minister Winston Churchill during World War II, securing the presidential role as a leader in international affairs.

Security Council (NSC). Truman also helped form the North Atlantic Treaty Organization (NATO), a mutual-protection alliance among Western nations.

Dwight D. Eisenhower, who succeeded Truman in 1953, did little to expand presidential power. He believed that the president should act strictly within constitutional guidelines and respect the powers of other government branches. Ironically, Eisenhower had his greatest impact on the presidency while he was not technically acting as president. In September 1955, he suffered a heart attack. During the several months that it took him to recover, Vice-president Richard M. Nixon ran the government as a caretaker. Confusion about who should fulfill Eisenhower's duties during his illness became a significant factor in formulating the Twenty-fifth Amendment; among other provisions, the amendment describes the process by which a president is to be replaced if he becomes incapacitated while in office.

The man who succeeded Eisenhower in 1961, John F. Kennedy, occupied the presidency for only 34 months, so his impact on the office was minimal. Nevertheless, as the first Catholic president, he broke through a religious barrier that until then had characterized the presidency. He was also the first chief executive to use television effectively to win supporters during the presidential campaign. In his 1960 television debates with Richard Nixon, Kennedy appeared confident, knowledgeable, and relaxed, while his opponent seemed ill at ease, defensive, and unprepared; many believe that Kennedy's victories in these encounters helped tip the balance in the closely contested race.

Kennedy also altered the public's perception of the chief executive. An immensely popular president, Kennedy fostered a close relationship between

Dwight D. Eisenhower (seated) recuperating from his heart attack in 1955. Confusion about who should fulfill his duties while he recovered raised questions about presidential succession.

55

Presidential candidate Richard Nixon (right) responds to John F. Kennedy during the 1960 television debates that helped Kennedy win the presidency.

the public and the first family. When he was assassinated in 1963, many Americans compared his loss to a death in the family.

The Imperial Presidency

During the administrations of Lyndon B. Johnson (1963–1969) and Richard M. Nixon (1969–1974), crises shook the presidency and transformed the American public's way of thinking about presidential power. The United States's involvement in the Vietnam War, which began during Eisenhower's administration, gained momentum under Kennedy, and escalated during the Johnson years, made many Americans question whether the president's powers in foreign affairs extended too far. Many worried that the president had obtained unrestricted authority to impose, without congressional approval, an American presence any place on the globe, a state of affairs historian Arthur M. Schlesinger, jr., later called the "imperial presidency."

Johnson seemed to lend credence to the idea of the "imperial presidency" when he sent troops to Vietnam without first gaining congressional approval. The public reacted so strongly against Johnson for escalating the Vietnam War that he declined to run for reelection in 1968.

President Richard M. Nixon, inaugurated in 1969, continued the pattern of making military decisions without consulting Congress. Like Johnson, he concealed facts about the war from Congress and the American people, including information about secret bombing raids on Cambodia. The apparent abuses of presidential power during the Vietnam War led Congress to pass the

Lyndon B. Johnson shows the strain of office as he prepares a major 1968 address on the Vietnam War. Because of public outcry over his escalation of the war, he decided not to run for reelection.

War Powers Act in 1973. This act restricted the president's power to send troops overseas and granted Congress the authority to order the president to remove troops.

By far the greatest blow to the imperial presidency was the Watergate scandal. On June 17, 1972, five men working for Nixon's reelection committee were arrested after breaking into the Democratic National Committee headquarters at the Watergate office complex in Washington, D.C. Using sophisticated equipment, they had photographed the office and planted listening devices that enabled them to eavesdrop on the campaign staff of George McGovern, Nixon's opponent in the 1972 election. At first, the arrests attracted little attention. The men refused to reveal for whom they were working, and the incident was overshadowed by the presidential campaign. But subsequent investigations by newspaper reporters, Justice Department lawyers, special prosecutors, grand juries, and congressional committees revealed not only the affiliation of the burglars but a pattern of corrupt and unlawful

Public opposition to the Vietnam War often led to violent protest. Here, Chicago police and National Guardsmen clash with demonstrators outside the Democratic National Convention in 1968.

Demonstrators show their support of the movement to impeach Nixon at a rally in front of the White House in October 1973. Nixon's role in the Watergate scandal seriously undermined the presidency.

activities that went far beyond the burglary. Investigators discovered that Nixon's campaign and presidential staffs had committed a long series of crimes—including other burglaries, bribery, accepting illegal campaign contributions, obstructing justice, and spying on political enemies.

Initially, Nixon's role in the crimes was not clear. But in the summer of 1973, former White House counsel John Dean told a Senate investigating committee that the president had known from the beginning about his staff's attempt to cover up illegal campaign activities. Congress then subpoenaed recordings of Nixon's conversations with his advisers, convinced that the tapes would corroborate Dean's testimony. Nixon refused to hand over the tapes, claiming "executive privilege"—the right to withhold internal communications that would adversely affect the executive office's function. On July 24, 1974, in the case of the *United States v. Nixon*, the Supreme Court ruled that Nixon had to release the tapes. Three days later, the House Judiciary Committee issued a report recommending that the House of Representatives bring a bill of impeachment against the president on three charges: obstruction of justice, abuse of presidential power, and refusal to obey congressional subpoenas. On August 9, 1974, Nixon resigned from office.

The Watergate hearings and Nixon's subsequent resignation forced Congress to severely limit presidential authority. During the presidencies of Gerald R. Ford (1974–1977) and Jimmy Carter (1977–1981), Congress restricted the chief executive's emergency powers, sought more control over the national budget and intelligence operations, vetoed more than 100 presidential measures, and rejected more presidential appointees than ever before.

In the 1980s, however, the presidency experienced a resurgence in power. The politically skillful and popular Ronald Reagan, who became president in 1981, enjoyed a friendly relationship with Congress and the courts. During his first term, the courts declared the legislative veto unconstitutional. At the same time, Congress hesitated to use the War Powers Act, slackened its supervision of intelligence agencies, and rarely rejected presidential appointees. During Reagan's second term, however, events such as the secret sale

Former White House counsel John Dean is sworn in on June 25, 1973, to testify before the Senate committee investigating the Watergate scandal. Dean alleged that Nixon had known of the cover-up from the beginning.

Ronald Reagan chats with workers during a tour of a Florida factory. The charismatic leader helped the presidency enjoy a resurgence of power in the 1980s.

of arms to Iran and the diversion of funds to Nicaragua's *Contra* rebels forced Congress to regulate White House activities more closely.

Since the days of George Washington the power of the presidency has relied more heavily on the personality of the man who holds the office than on the Constitution's sketchy guidelines. In modern times, the president's popularity and political skill have played an increasing role in enlarging presidential power. Each president has molded the office to some extent, and almost every administration has altered the internal function—and the public perception—of the presidency.

The White House serves as the home of the first family as well as the headquarters for nearly 400 people who work in the Executive Office.

FIVE

The Structure of the Executive Office

The president administers the executive branch of the government, which includes the Executive Office of the President, 13 executive departments, and numerous agencies. Traditionally, executive department heads and the vice-president compose the president's cabinet. In the nation's early years, cabinet members were the presidents' most important advisers. This tradition gave way with the presidency of Andrew Jackson, who relied heavily on a group of unofficial advisers known as the "Kitchen Cabinet." Since then presidents have continued to seek the counsel of personal advisers as well as cabinet members.

The degree to which the president interacts with his staff varies greatly from one administration to the next. For example, Richard Nixon tended to close off his office even to members of his cabinet. Many of his assistants seldom saw him. In contrast, Jimmy Carter made a special effort to keep his administration open and relaxed, seeking to be known as what he called a "people's president." The amount of authority a president delegates to his staff also varies widely, not necessarily in relation to accessibility. For instance, even though Nixon was extremely inaccessible, he allowed members of his personal staff a great deal of independence in initiating policy. Carter, on the other hand, preferred a "hands-on" management style: For example, he insisted on reading every paper on important issues rather than relying on presidential briefings.

The Executive Office

At the heart of the Executive Office are the approximately 400 people who work in the White House itself. The most influential members of this group are the chief of staff and the counsel to the president, who advise the president and direct the other White House staff members. Of almost equal importance are the press secretary and the deputy press secretary, who arrange press conferences and frequently speak to the press on the president's behalf; the legislative strategy coordinator, who helps the president formulate legislation; and the communications director, who oversees the writing of the president's speeches and issues policy statements. Other members of the Executive Office include the assistants to the president for political and governmental

Deputy Press Secretary Larry Speakes addresses members of the press at a 1986 briefing. The press secretary organizes press conferences and issues statements on the president's behalf.

David Stockman, director of the Office of Management and Budget, prepares to brief senators on the proposed 1984 federal budget.

affairs, special support services, legislative affairs, national security affairs, and policy development.

The Executive Office includes a number of agencies directed by the president. The most important of these, the National Security Council (NSC), oversees and coordinates the work of the intelligence and defense agencies. The president chairs the NSC. Its other members include the secretary of state, the secretary of defense, the director of the office of emergency planning, the chairman of the Joint Chiefs of Staff, and the director of the Central Intelligence Agency (CIA).

The largest executive agency, the Office of Management and Budget (OMB), prepares the annual federal budget that the president submits to Congress. Each year, the OMB estimates what the government's tax revenues will be and how much money the government will need to operate. It also monitors congressional expenditures, analyzes the effectiveness of government programs, and coordinates the policies of government agencies.

The executive office also includes six smaller departments designed to assist the chief executive. Among these departments is the Office of Policy

Development, which helps the president devise and coordinate domestic strategy in such diverse areas as farm policy, community development, and school lunches. Its 45 staff members also advise the president's cabinet.

Another executive department, the Council of Economic Advisers, keeps the president informed about the state of the nation's economy and helps prepare his annual economic report to Congress. The council, composed of three presidentially appointed economists and a small staff, recommends policies to aid national economic growth and stability.

The Office of Science and Technology Policy advises the president on scientific, engineering, and technological matters that affect the nation. Its director, chosen by the president with the Senate's consent, manages a staff of 11 analysts and a budget of more than $1.9 million. The office researches such

Ronald Reagan (second from left) meets with his cabinet in November 1985. The cabinet serves as the president's informal advisory board.

topics as solar energy and space travel and publishes reports relating to science policy.

The Council of Environmental Quality monitors the nation's environment for the president. This council also prepares on behalf of the president an annual state-of-the-environment report to Congress. Like the Council of Economic Advisers, it consists of three presidentially appointed members and a small staff.

The president's chief adviser on foreign trade policy heads the Office of the United States Trade Representative. The trade representative holds the rank of ambassador and represents the country in all foreign trade negotiations. This department's annual budget exceeds $10 million and its staff numbers 115.

The Office of Administration assists each of the units of the Executive Office, providing data processing, clerical, and library services (except to the president himself, who has his own support staff). The administration office receives a budget of more than $13.1 million and has a staff of almost 150.

The Cabinet

The executive branch contains 13 executive departments whose leaders serve as the cabinet—the president's informal advisory board. In addition, the president can accord cabinet rank to other executive branch officials, such as the vice-president or the director of the CIA. The president appoints each cabinet secretary with the approval of the Senate.

The secretary of state acts as the president's chief diplomatic representative, conducting negotiations with other countries and protecting the foreign interests of the United States. Aside from the president, the secretary of state is probably the most well-known American diplomat. Some secretaries of state, such as Henry Kissinger, became world-famous through their diplomatic negotiations.

The defense secretary heads a huge defense establishment that includes more than 3 million military and civilian employees. He advises the president on such matters as weapons systems, military preparedness, and foreign troop strength. He often works closely with the secretary of state in sensitive weapons negotiations.

The president's chief economic adviser—the secretary of the treasury—oversees the Treasury Department's varied functions. This department includes the Internal Revenue Service, the United States Mint, the Customs Service, the United States Secret Service, and the Bureau of Alcohol, Tobacco and Firearms.

Henry Kissinger (right) confers with Richard M. Nixon in 1972. As secretary of state, Kissinger strengthened diplomatic ties with American allies and opened talks with China and the Soviet Union.

Franklin D. Roosevelt (seated, center) poses with his cabinet in 1936. The president's cabinet consists of the heads of each of the federal executive-branch departments.

The attorney general leads the Department of Justice, which advises the president on legal issues and represents the government in court. The attorney general also oversees the Justice Department's various units, including the Federal Bureau of Investigation, the Drug Enforcement Administration, the Immigration and Naturalization Service, and the Bureau of Prisons.

The secretary of the interior directs the huge Department of the Interior, which is responsible for administering more than 500 million acres of federal land, including the national parks. The department also oversees the allocation and conservation of natural resources. The secretary acts as the president's chief source of information on the nation's water, mineral, forest, fish, and wildlife resources.

The secretary of agriculture oversees the nation's farm-related activities, ranging from farm loans to soil conservation. One of his department's major responsibilities is monitoring the quality of the nation's food supply. The agriculture secretary also administers food assistance services such as the food stamp program.

Two departments, the Department of Commerce and the Department of Labor, once formed a single agency. Today, however, the secretary of commerce reports to the president on matters of trade, business, and industry. The secretary of labor advises the president on labor-related matters, such as employment statistics and occupational health and safety concerns.

Some cabinet members spend more time working for the public than advising the president. For example, the secretary of health and human services administers such services as Social Security benefits, Aid to Families with Dependent Children (welfare), Medicare, and Medicaid. The secretary of housing and urban development assists citizens through housing programs, such as the Government National Mortgage Association and the Fair Housing and Equal Opportunity program.

The secretary of transportation directs such agencies as the United States Coast Guard, the Federal Aviation Administration, and the National Highway Traffic Safety Administration, which oversee the safety of public travel. The secretary of energy oversees the nation's fuel needs, including the utilization of nuclear energy. The secretary of education promotes public education and enforces federal guidelines on equal education opportunity.

Each of these cabinet secretaries informs the president of the major foreign and domestic challenges facing his administration. Although some presidents have not relied upon their cabinets as heavily as others, cabinet members have always influenced national policy to some degree.

Anatomy of a Campaign: Carter in 1976

Every four years since 1824 the Democratic and Republican parties have held national conventions, where groups of delegates from every state gather to vote for their party's presidential nominee. A portion of these delegates are appointed by state and local party officials, who trust them to vote for the candidate the officials prefer. The rest are elected by the party's members in primaries—preliminary elections held in several states—and are thereby committed to vote at the convention for the candidate the voters prefer.

Until recently, primaries played only a minor role in the nominating process; at most, 40 percent of delegates were bound by primary results. But in 1970, the system changed. Antiwar Democrats, upset that their party had chosen Hubert Humphrey as their 1968 presidential nominee even though he had not won a single primary, secured major changes in the party's nomination rules. Under the new system, the proportion of delegates bound by primary results to vote for a particular candidate jumped to 70 percent. This gave the voters a much greater say in selecting their party's nominee. It also dramatically increased the importance of the primary elections.

Jimmy Carter was the first candidate to take full advantage of the new system. Before the 1976 campaign, Carter was virtually unknown to the American people. He had no experience in national affairs and few allies among the Democratic party leadership. But his shrewd campaign strategy enabled him to win 17 of the 30 primaries and to secure his party's nomination earlier than any candidate had for many years. The following chronology outlines the key events in Carter's primary campaign.

◆ ◆ ◆ ◆ ◆

1/1/76: As the year begins, nine candidates have entered the Democratic race. Carter's moderate political views set him apart from his opponents, who include conservative Alabama governor George Wallace and an ample field of liberals— among them Arizona representative Morris Udall and Washington senator Henry M. Jackson. Minnesota senator Hubert H. Humphrey has not officially entered the race, but says he would accept the nomination if it were offered to him.

So far Carter has done poorly in the polls. A Gallup poll shows him as the favorite of only 4 percent of the electorate. But aides are hopeful that aggressive campaigning will begin to pay off in the primaries. By this time, he has already traveled to 37 states, delivered more than 100 speeches, and appeared on 93 radio and television broadcasts. Carter plans to run in every primary, placing emphasis on the early contests, which, though they do not involve a large number of delegates, receive exaggerated attention from the press. If he can establish himself as the frontrunner with a few early victories, then he will be guaranteed

After winning the Wisconsin primary, Carter holds aloft a copy of a Milwaukee newspaper that prematurely declared Morris Udall the victor.

extensive media coverage for the duration of the campaign.

1/19/76: Carter wins the Iowa caucuses, receiving the support of 27.6 percent of Democrats designating a favorite. United Press International and *Time* magazine point to Carter as the potential frontrunner and increase the number of reporters assigned to cover his campaign.

2/24/76: Carter wins the New Hampshire primary with 28.4 percent of the vote. Shortly thereafter, he appears on the covers of *Time* and *Newsweek*.

3/4/76: Carter wins the Florida primary, receiving 34.3 percent of the vote to Wallace's 30.6 percent. His victory proves that he can compete with Wallace in the South.

4/24/76: Carter wins the Pennsylvania primary. An exit poll (a poll of voters as they leave voting precincts) demonstrates the value of his extensive press coverage: 25 percent of the voters say that Carter's was the only name on the ballot they

recognized. Afterward, Carter announces that he will cut back on campaigning to prepare for the general election. By this time, three of the original nine candidates have quit the race.

5/76: Carter receives strong challenges from two latecomers to the campaign, losing in Nebraska to Idaho senator Frank Church and in Maryland to California governor Edmund G. Brown, Jr.

6/8/76: Carter loses the California and New Jersey primaries but captures 52 percent of the Ohio vote. By this time, his delegates total 1,117—388 short of the number required for the nomination. Within the next few weeks, Carter's opposition collapses; his remaining opponents release their delegates and offer full support.

7/14/76: Carter wins the Democratic presidential nomination on the first ballot of the convention.

Joining hands with his wife Rosalynn and his running mate, Minnesota senator Walter Mondale, Jimmy Carter (center) celebrates his nomination as presidential candidate at the 1976 Democratic National Convention.

Independent Agencies

The executive branch also includes more than 200 independent agencies that vary in size, function, and degree of presidential control. For example, the president directly oversees some executive agencies, such as the National Aeronautics and Space Administration (NASA) and the Small Business Administration. Others, such as the Federal Trade Commission and the board of governors of the Federal Reserve System, do not fall under the president's immediate jurisdiction, although he appoints their members with the Senate's consent. Still others, such as the Federal Deposit Insurance Corporation (FDIC) and the United States Postal Service, are governed by congressional charter. The president must receive Senate approval to appoint their top officers, as he must for all high-level appointees.

Running for Office

The campaign for the presidency generally begins more than two years before the election, when candidates formally announce that they intend to seek their political party's nomination. Most candidates apply for the nomination early so they have time to raise sufficient campaign funds. Early application also lets them participate in straw votes (informal votes that gauge the strength of opposing candidates or issues) and caucuses (party meetings to determine a candidate's strength or to select delegates to the state or national convention).

The next step involves primary elections, in which candidates vie for the support of delegates to their party's national convention. Some primaries are restricted to party members; others are open to all registered voters. Generally, the percentage of votes that a candidate receives in a state primary determines the number of delegates from that state who will support that candidate at the convention. At the same time, candidates try to influence state caucuses, where the orientation of many other delegates is determined. By the end of primary season, the majority of delegates are committed to one of the candidates, though a significant minority remain uncommitted. (The number of uncommitted delegates at conventions has recently decreased as a result of the increase in the number of primaries.) Eventually, each party holds a state convention to make its final delegate selection. These delegates then go on to the national convention.

National conventions, held during the summer of the election year, perform four major functions. They adopt a party platform, which defines campaign issues and party philosophy; they create policies and procedures to govern

Nixon kicks off his 1968 presidential campaign in Chicago. Presidential candidates travel around the country talking to voters and participating in party rallies and parades.

the next convention; they rally support for party candidates and encourage party solidarity; and finally, they nominate the party's presidential and vice-presidential candidates.

Shortly after the convention, the candidates begin their final campaigns. For two months, they travel around the country, raising money and organizing staffs who will gather crowds, distribute literature, create publicity, research issues, and produce campaign paraphernalia. The candidates must persuade local politicians to campaign for them and charm the media into giving them wide and favorable coverage. They must also deal with any potentially damaging revelations.

On Election Day—the first Tuesday after the first Monday in November of an election year—voters in each state cast their ballots. When the electoral college meets in December, each state elector casts a ballot for the candidate who received the majority of the votes in his or her state. (Although electors are not legally bound to vote for the candidate who won in their state, they are honor bound to do so.)

Delegates crowd the floor of the 1956 Republican National Convention. At national conventions, delegates nominate the party's presidential and vice-presidential candidates.

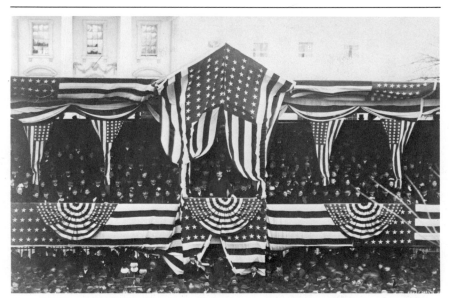

Grover Cleveland's 1893 inauguration ceremony. Presidential election results go into effect when the president is inaugurated on January 20 of the year following the election.

The electoral college system makes it possible for a candidate to win a majority of electoral votes without having won a majority of popular votes. Three times in American history—in 1824, 1876, and 1888—the electoral college has selected a candidate who received fewer popular votes than another candidate. Because of this possibility, Congress has repeatedly attempted to abolish the electoral college. Nevertheless, the system has endured.

Presidential election results become official in January of the year following an election, when Congress convenes to open the electoral ballots. Finally, on January 20 of the year following the election, the chief justice of the United States inaugurates the new president and vice-president by administering their oaths of office.

The president's job has grown much more complex since the Constitution defined the office in 1787. This 1961 photograph of John F. Kennedy in the Oval Office epitomizes the burdens of the modern presidency.

SIX

The President's Many Roles

Article II of the U.S. Constitution grants the president an array of specific powers and responsibilities. But the authority granted to the modern presidency far exceeds the constitutional definition of the office. Through the years, a variety of presidential roles have evolved that were not specifically outlined in Article II. Congress legislated some of these roles, the courts granted some, and powerful presidents assumed others.

The president's first role is as chief executive, the "boss" of the executive branch and most of its workers. He is responsible for the ethics, loyalty, efficiency, and responsiveness of the federal government and its employees. The evolution of the chief executive's primary role provides a useful example of how presidential power has developed through the years. At the outset, the Constitution granted the chief executive the power to appoint all officials in the executive branch. After George Washington's term, custom gave the chief executive the power to remove appointees. Finally, legislation granted him the power to reorganize agencies and to prepare budgets.

In the role of chief of state, the president acts as ceremonial head of the federal government. In this capacity, the president must greet distinguished visitors, bestow medals, and host state dinners. Or as President William Howard Taft once said, the president must act as "the personal embodiment

As ceremonial head of the federal government, President Nixon hosts a banquet for Chinese premier Chou En-Lai during his 1972 tour of China.

and representative of [the] dignity and majesty" of the people, government, and laws of the United States.

The president also serves as commander in chief of the nation's armed forces, which makes him ultimately responsible for the nation's defense. As commander in chief, he appoints and removes generals, makes key military decisions (such as when and where to wage war), and negotiates armistice terms. During wartime emergencies, the commander in chief is entitled to restrict civil liberties, to exert greater control over the economy, to seize industries, to fix wages and prices, and to settle labor disputes. Finally, the commander in chief alone decides when and if the nation will use its atomic weapons.

The president plays another important role as the nation's chief diplomat. Although the Constitution attempted to divide diplomatic affairs between the president and Congress, these affairs have become primarily a presidential responsibility. The president negotiates treaties and executive agreements, manages foreign alliances, recognizes new governments, appoints and supervises diplomatic personnel, and receives foreign ambassadors.

The Constitution accords the president the power to veto congressional bills and recommend legislation to Congress. If the president disapproves of a bill, he can respond with a "message veto" and return the bill to Congress with a message stating his reasons for not signing it. Or, if Congress is about to adjourn, the president can respond with a "pocket veto" and refuse to sign the bill within 10 days. (If Congress adjourns within that time, the bill will not become law.) In modern times, the president not only recommends a large portion of the country's legislation but drafts it as well. The president also has a responsibility to the legislature: He must annually address Congress on the state of the Union.

The roles of chief executive, chief of state, commander in chief, chief diplomat, and a key legislator originated in the Constitution. But over time, the presidency has acquired many other roles that the Constitution's framers never imagined. One of these is the role of party chief. Today, a candidate must have his political party's full support in order to become president. Once elected, a president must become a skillful party leader to use the party's power to achieve his goals. Therefore, presidents court the favor of party members in Congress and place fellow party members in important government posts.

The president's role as national spokesman also evolved through the years.

In this 1928 cartoon, Uncle Sam enlarges the "presidential chair" to accommodate the president's increasing responsibilities.

At home, the president speaks for the nation's ideals; abroad, he embodies American beliefs. Modern presidents have been especially effective in this role because they have had almost unlimited access to the mass media and have commanded a huge government information network.

The role of chief of the nation's economy is another informal presidential function. The president must submit a report to Congress each year detailing national economic statistics and suggesting ways to stimulate the economy. The president can influence the economy through tax policy, the military establishment (the nation's largest single consumer), and public relief agencies, such as the Social Security and Veterans administrations. Furthermore, the president appoints the members of economic regulatory agencies, such as the Federal Reserve Board.

The president can also affect the world economy through control of foreign trade. In addition to his extensive formal powers over tariff rates and quotas, he has a variety of informal powers. He can generate adverse publicity against nations and their industries. He can even instruct the Justice Department to enforce economic laws against those nations and industries that do not cooperate with his policies.

President Reagan (center) poses with foreign leaders at the 1987 economic summit conference in Venice. The president can affect the world economy through his control of foreign trade.

Ronald Reagan (second from right) meets with Soviet leader Mikhail Gorbachev (left) in October 1986. In discussions with Communist leaders, the U.S. president represents all nations belonging to the North Atlantic Treaty Organization (NATO).

Most modern presidents have also assumed the role of peacekeeper. At home, the president can employ federal marshals to protect the peace and, in case of riots, can call out the National Guard or the Army. Abroad, he can use American troops to enforce the peace in war-torn countries. At home and abroad, he can call on various government organizations to alleviate suffering and prevent looting after natural disasters.

Finally, the president functions as a world leader. In discussions with Communist nations, he acts not only as America's chief executive but also as the leader of nations belonging to NATO. Many of his other functions, such as controller of America's atomic arsenal, give him great power over millions of people around the world. The Constitution and federal laws serve to keep the president's authority in check.

Limits on Presidential Power

In addition to direct constitutional restraints, various judicial and legislative actions indirectly check presidential power. For example, the courts have restricted the president's authority to abridge civil rights and to seize industries during emergencies.

Congress can use a number of formal and informal tools to recapture power from the president. Legislators can investigate alleged wrongdoing by a president or his administration or refuse to approve presidential legislation. They can also legislate specific qualifications for some presidential appointees, and they have imposed laws forbidding a president to remove appointees from office arbitrarily. In addition, Congress can deny funds for presidential programs. The Senate can halt the legislative process with filibusters (nonstop speech-making that delays congressional business). Congressional leaders can also challenge the president by voting to override a presidential veto of a bill. If at least two-thirds of the members of each house vote to override the veto, the bill becomes law.

Other groups also have the power to hinder presidential plans. Government agencies and bureaus can frustrate executive power by neglecting to support or execute presidential programs. State and local governments can thwart the president by failing to enforce federal rules or by observing the letter but not the spirit of federal guidelines.

John F. Kennedy is photographed accepting his party's nomination as presidential candidate in 1960. Modern politicians must use the media effectively to present their ideas and programs to the public.

Former national security adviser Robert C. McFarlane (left) is sworn in before a congressional committee during the 1987 hearings to investigate the government's secret sale of arms to Iran and the diversion of funds to Nicaragua's Contra rebels.

But by far the most effective limits on presidential power come from the American people. A president who is concerned about his political future—or the future of his party—cannot extend his power beyond that granted by the people. Concern about the judgment of history also restricts political activities. No president wants to be recorded as the first American dictator.

83

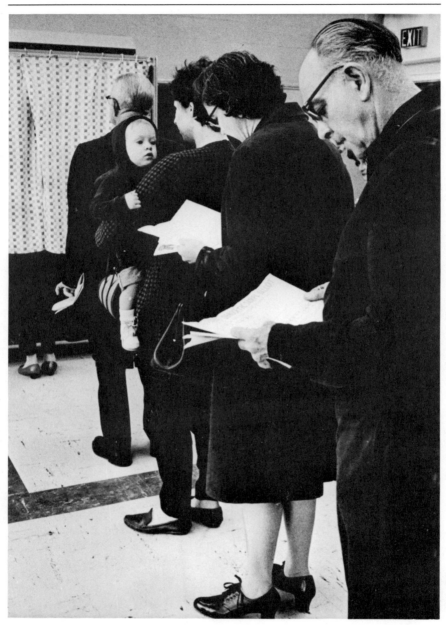

By voting in elections, American citizens are able to choose a presidential candidate whose political views are compatible with their own.

SEVEN

Prospects for the Presidency

Since colonial days Americans have questioned the wisdom of concentrating power in the hands of a president. The notion of executive authority appears somehow contrary to democratic ideals. Yet the complexity of federal government seems to require that someone hold ultimate responsibility for the nation. America's early leaders designated the president as this final authority.

At the Constitutional Convention in 1787, delegate Gouverneur Morris cautioned, "Make [the president] too weak: the Legislature will usurp his power. Make him too strong: he will usurp on the Legislature." Heeding this warning, the delegates created an office that was part of a system of checks and balances. Yet the presidency's strength has been determined largely by those who have held the position. During more than 200 years, presidents weak and strong have molded the office.

Fluctuations in presidential strength have proved that the Constitution is a dynamic charter capable of protecting America from both weakness and tyranny. When the presidency loses too much power, a strong president can reassert its authority; when it becomes too strong, Congress and the people can check its power.

In the 20th century, the president's powers have exceeded the framers' expectations. Since World War II the United States and its president have moved into the forefront of world events. By virtue of their office, even weak or unpopular presidents have gained tremendous power to shape world events and opinions. Of course, this power has carried with it great responsibility.

From the executive office's beginning, presidents have felt the burden of their position. John Adams noted that "no man who ever held the office would congratulate a friend on attaining it." As presidential power has expanded, the responsibilities have grown even greater. As technological advances and social conditions seem to make the world grow smaller, the president's role will continue to expand. Advances in weaponry will increase the chance of nuclear war and add to the president's overwhelming responsibility to maintain peace. As the population of the United States and the world continues to spiral upward, the president will face the continued challenge of providing adequate jobs, food, and housing.

American schoolchildren pledge their allegiance to the nation's flag.
Future generations of voters will continue to shape the presidency.

Like its past, the presidency's future will depend largely on those who hold the office. Future chief executives will continue to shape the presidency through their perception of the role and their ability to attain and hold power. Like their predecessors, future presidents will continue to mold the office to suit their personalities, political philosophies, and policy goals.

Ultimately, however, the American people are responsible for shaping the presidency's future. To protect democracy, Americans must examine and understand the Constitution and the nation's laws. They must participate in the electoral process by examining the issues, making informed decisions, and exercising their right to vote. Finally, Americans must vigilantly guard their freedoms to ensure that presidents maintain the fine balance between authority and oppression. For as Abraham Lincoln said more than a century ago, "Our reliance against tyranny is the love of liberty."

Agencies of the Executive Office

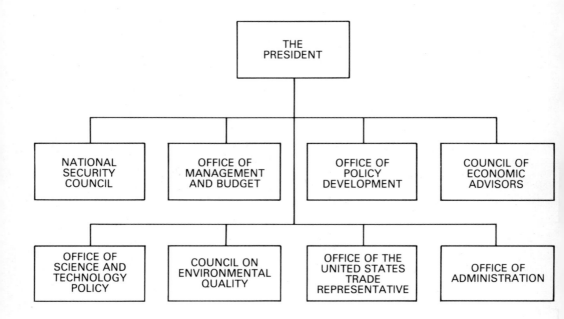

The President's Cabinet

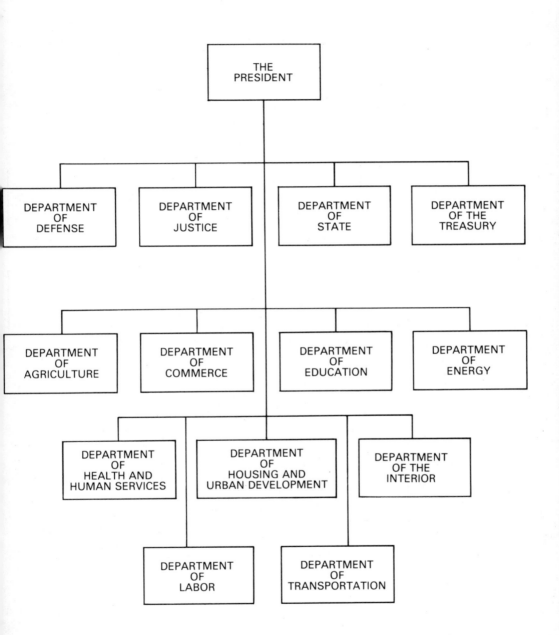

GLOSSARY

Articles of Confederation   The first official charter of the United States. Ratified in 1781, it granted sole governing authority to Congress.

Australian ballot   A ballot printed at public expense that lists all candidates, regardless of party, and provides voter secrecy. First used during William McKinley's 1896 presidential election.

Cabinet   A panel of the president's closest advisers.

Caucus   A closed meeting of members of a political party to select candidates or decide policy.

Checks and balances   Division of power among the executive, legislative, and judicial branches of government to insure that no single branch becomes too powerful.

Electoral college   A body of state representatives (electors) that casts ballots to determine the winners of a presidential election.

Executive privilege   The presidential right to withhold from investigators internal communications that would hinder the functions of the executive office.

Impeachment   An action of Congress charging the president, vice-president, or other civil official with treason, bribery, or other high crimes.

Implied powers   Powers assumed by the president that the Constitution does not specifically grant.

Incumbent   The current occupant of an office.

National convention   A meeting held during the summer of an election year by each political party in order to adopt a party platform and nominate the party's presidential and vice-presidential candidates.

Party platform   A statement of principles and policies adopted by a political party.

Prerogative power Divine authority to govern, believed to belong to a monarch or his appointees.

Primary election An election in which presidential candidates vie for their party's nomination. Some primaries are open only to party members; others are open to all registered voters.

Spoils system Political patronage system in which a successful candidate rewards supporters with government appointments on the basis of party membership or political loyalty.

Straw vote An informal vote that gauges the strength of opposing candidates or issues.

SELECTED REFERENCES

Baily, Thomas A. *Presidential Greatness: The Image and the Man from George Washington to the Present.* New York: Appleton-Century-Crofts, 1966.

Burns, James MacGregor. *Presidential Government: The Crucible of Leadership.* Boston: Houghton Mifflin, 1966.

Collier, Christopher, and James Lincoln Collier. *Decision in Philadelphia: The Constitutional Convention of 1787.* New York: Random House, 1986.

Kane, Joseph N. *Facts About the President.* 4th ed. New York: H. W. Wilson, 1981.

Koenig, Louis W. *The Chief Executive.* New York: Harcourt, Brace and World, 1964.

LeLoup, Lance T. *Politics in America: The Ability to Govern.* St. Paul: West Publishing Co., 1986.

Leuchtenburg, William E. *In the Shadow of FDR: From Harry Truman to Ronald Reagan.* Ithaca, N.Y.: Cornell University Press, 1985.

McCormick, Richard P. *The Presidential Game: The Origins of American Presidential Politics.* New York: Oxford University Press, 1982.

Nash, Bradley D., et al. *Organizing and Staffing the Presidency.* Center for the Study of the Presidency: Proceedings: Volume III, Number 1, 1979.

Pious, Richard M. *The American Presidency.* New York: Basic Books, 1979.

Schlesinger, Arthur M., jr. *The Imperial Presidency.* Boston: Houghton Mifflin, 1973.

Tebbel, John, and Sarah Miles Watts. *The Press and the Presidency: From George Washington to Ronald Reagan.* New York: Oxford University Press, 1985.

Tugwell, Rexford G. *How They Became President.* New York: Simon & Schuster, 1964.

The United States Government Manual 1986/87. Office of the Federal Register, National Archives and Records Services. Washington, D.C.: U.S. Government Printing Office, 1984.

White, Theodore H. *America in Search of Itself: The Making of the President, 1956–1980.* New York: Harper & Row, 1982.

INDEX

Christine Brendel Scriabine is a historical consultant based in Connecticut. She holds a Ph.D. from Brown University, has been a member of the faculty at Pennsylvania State University, and has served as historian for the University of Hartford's Museum of American Political Life. Her published articles have addressed the presidency, Connecticut history, and social history issues.

Arthur M. Schlesinger, jr., served in the White House as special assistant to Presidents Kennedy and Johnson. He is the author of numerous acclaimed works in American history and has twice been awarded the Pulitzer Prize. He taught history at Harvard College for many years and is currently Albert Schweitzer Professor of the Humanities at the City College of New York.

The White House, 1600 Pennsylvania Avenue, N.W., Washington, D.C., 202-456-1414. The president's home attracts more than 2 million visitors a year. It is open to the public Tuesday through Saturday, 10:00 A.M. to 12:00 P.M., and is closed on Thanksgiving and Christmas. The free tour includes a lecture and a visit to the five state rooms. Tickets can be obtained on the day of the tour at the East Gate visitor's entrance on East Executive Avenue.

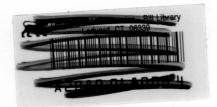
DATE DUE

SEP 4 1996		
SEP 17 1996		
FEB 13 2001		
OCT 27 2008		

Demco, Inc. 38-293